DON HANFORD
1/15/97

# Goodguys
# Hot Rod
# Chronicles

Thaxton Press

First published in 1996 by Thaxton Press, PO Box 1742, Sebastopol, California. 95473 USA

The information in this book is true and complete to the best of our knowledge. All recommendations are made without any guarantee on the part of the author or Publisher, who also disclaim any liability incurred in connection with the use of this publication.

We recognize that some words, model names and designations, for example, mentioned herein are the property of the trademark holder. We use them for identification purposes only. This is not an official publication. ® Goodguys and their association logos are registered and copyrighted trademarks of Goodguys, Alamo California.

Printed in Hong Kong

Library of Congress Cataloging-in Publication Data Available
96-60750

ISBN 0-9652005-4-X

**On the front cover:** Gary's new ' 47 Plymouth is his everyday driver. Insert: This photo of Ernie Hashim from the 1959 Fuel and Gas Championships in Bakersfield is one of the most memorable drag racing events of all time. The finals were run in near darkness on Sunday night as racers paired off for the Championship.

**On the frontispiece:** In 1956 and 1957 I used to attend every drag race and speedway race I could and I always took along my camera. I enjoyed the Visalia Airport drags run by the Vapor Trailers Hot Rod Club because of the variety of machines that ran at this event. This Model A Competition roadster, raced by the Smokers out of Bakersfield, was powered by a '55 Pontiac as I recall, and featured flat alloy wheel discs and a hooped roll bar.

**On the title page:** This photo of the Plymouth was taken just after my first Kingsburg Car Show. It had scallops, wide whites, Olds Fiesta hubcaps and it was lowered. I had already cut the coils and used lowering blocks in the rear, but I added a set of dumbbells to the trunk just to get it down a little more.

# Contents

Dedication:
Bruce Olson 1939 -1990
This book is dedicated to my hot rod friend Bruce Olson—A real hot rodding "Goodguy."

Gary Meadors

# Introduction

Welcome to The Goodguys Hot Rod Chronicles. Within these pages is a brief history of the Meadors family and the story of the Goodguys organization which flowered, under the care and management of Gary and Marilyn Meadors, into the world's leading hot rod event company.

Often copied, but never matched, the Goodguys organization has its roots in the "American Graffiti" life of Gary Meadors who grew up only forty miles from where George Lucas experienced the same life and used it to create his classic cruisin' movie.

Gary's passion for lowered rods and auto racing is confirmed by his vintage photo library from which the vast majority of these photos have been taken. His talent with the camera recorded what he saw and enjoyed, and later gave him the confidence to produce stories for major hot rodding magazines.

Gary has allowed us to look back over his young years as a rural kid from the tiny town of Dinuba in the Central Valley of California revealing a slice of his and Marilyn's early family life. Gary's teenage years were full of enjoyable hot rodding experiences which enriched his life and lead him along a winding path to create the Goodguys which is now one of the most recognized names in the street rodding industry.

Where possible, we have used photographs not previously published and which provide an insight into why Gary has been able to create such a popular organization.

Thaxton Press would like to thank everyone who has been involved with this book, especially Bill "The Kid" Burnham for his great work on the history of the Goodguys and the Danville Dukes story, Greg Sharp of NHRA Historical Services for his eagle-eyed memories of hot rodding, John Drummond and Steve Anderson at Goodguys and, of course, Gary and Marilyn Meadors for their time and energy in getting this book wrapped up.

David Fetherston

## Acknowledgements
Thaxton Press would also like to thank these wonderful folks: Teka Luttrell for his input on the design and layout, Paragon 3 for their cover design work, Gloria Fetherston, and Nanette Simmons, at Simmons Editorial Services, for their work on production.

Right: Ya gotta love this wild looking '32 three-window coupe with its massive engine setback, zoomie headers, alloy wheels and Moon tank. I shot this Deuce at the First Fuel and Gas Championship at Bakersfield in early 1959. The coupe was raced by the Motor Monarchs from Ventura, California, and was powered by an Oldsmobile with a Cad transmission.

# Goodguys
# Hot Rod
# Chronicles

The History of Hot Rodding's First Family of Fun

# The Dinuba Kid

I grew up in the San Joaquin Valley, just a few miles south of Fresno, California in the farming metropolis of Dinuba. This township was probably only on the map because it was located at the intersection of the county road J19, and the 201 State Route. My brother and I were farm kids who helped our family in their struggle to raise cotton, corn, tomatoes, watermelon and cantaloupes on rented property.

I think I must have inherited my love of cars from my dad. He and his buddy, Cadamus, owned a stripped down Model T speedster. They'd drive the speedster up to General Grant Park in the nearby National Forest to race other guys with similar cars. He told me they'd race and roar downhill, squealing and screaming in those early days of hot rodding with nothing but mechanical brakes between them and

their maker.

Unlike me, dad was a patient man who could sit alone quietly building model airplanes or hand-tieing fishing flies for hours on end. He didn't need instant gratification. I had no time for such tedious stuff! I was out roaming around

Below: Glen Meadors, my dad, did some racing down Strawberry Grade in the twenties. The grade was so steep that they raced downhill instead of racing uphill! I think this is the first family roadster. The back of the photo says November 1933, a little before my time.

Series game. I guess it's one of those oddball memories that you retain. Church was a routine part of our lives and I regularly attended Sunday school, sang in the choir and yes, proudly earned my 12-year pin. I even played the trumpet religiously until I had to wear braces.

Dad would often tell me about his '35 Ford with checkers painted on the hood side panels which he'd spiffed up to impress my mom. She was a South Dakota preacher's daughter and became smitten by dad who was a fancy dressing dapper dancer. Dad was also an excellent spring board diver and I can recall people stopping to watch him perform a perfect Swan or Half Gainer from the diving board at the Dinuba Plunge. I was truly proud to see my dad silence the crowd and execute a perfect dive.

Below: I was on wheels early and I wish I still had this great looking wagon. The wagon was around the farm for years but, like all those old toys, it got handed on or trashed.

Above: In the summer, the Central Valley of California becomes an oven with daytime temperatures, in Dinuba, a scorching 100 degrees for many weeks. To get away from the heat, the family would drive across to Santa Cruz on the coast for the weekends. This shot from 1941 was on the beach just below the boardwalk in Santa Cruz and, boy, am I glad I don't have that "beer gut" anymore.

searching for things to do that kept me fired up and active. Granddad was still part of our lives. I remember hearing stories about him being a semi-pro baseball pitcher but then becoming a Mennonite preacher (a pretty strict religion). However, he never lost his love for the game; he'd come over to our house to watch baseball games on the TV but felt obliged to leave the room whenever the beer and cigarette commercials came on. I don't believe he ever missed an inning. I remember one time he showed up on a Sunday, most unusual for him, to watch a World

Above: Marilyn Jones was a twin - Carolyn Sue (L) and Marilyn Lou (R) at six months.

dots, and they raced it at the Dinuba Legion Bowl. I was in the Boy Scouts at the time and earned my admittance to the grandstands by selling soda pop. If you sold all your pop, then you could take a seat in the bleachers. I was always the first kid to sell my quota, being quite a hustling 12 year-old.

Come to think of it, that old Poncho wasn't very fast—I don't think they ever won a race—but it had huge 4-inch exhaust tubes and sounded outrageous.

Dad loved auto racing, too. He used to take me to the Fresno Airport to watch Eli and Billy Vukovich race Midgets. Dad even built a Go Kart, raced it several times and won a couple of races. He let me drive it occasionally but then I crashed it, and that was the end of that episode.

About this time my brother and I decided to adopt dad's old '41 Chevy sedan. The family already owned a work truck and mom drove a

My strongest automotive reminiscences of this time recall a neighbor of ours, Tom Cockran, who lived in the farm house just down the road and owned a '48 Dodge Club Coupe with a split exhaust manifold.

What a great sound that six-cylinder motor made, a lot more distinctive than the flathead V8's! He'd wind it up to about 50 mph then, just as he passed our place, he'd back off the gas. I'd actually lay awake at night waiting for him to pass by. That six cylinder serenading my ears had me vowing one day to own a sweet sounding car just like that. When Tom went off to join the Navy his younger brother, Buzz, took over the sound department with a '47 Plymouth coupe.

That influenced me so, that when I was old enough, you guessed it, I bought a Plymouth, too.

Tom and Buzz were my heroes. They built a jalopy racer from a '37 Pontiac. It had no fenders, no glass, was painted white with huge red polka

Above: A man of action on the pier at Santa Cruz.

'52 Lincoln as her work car, so the '41 was at our disposal. We'd use the Chevy, with the back seat and divider panel removed, to haul sweet corn from our farm to the grocery stores. What we couldn't sell to the stores we'd bring back home and then try to sell it from a stand in front of our house. The '41 Chevy was our first car experience and a '32 Ford Tudor was our second. It belonged to one of our hired hands who'd had it customized by kicking out the side glass so he could throw in his hoe and shovel. He let us use the car for an entire summer and allowed us to saw off the muffler and whack the floor shift lever way down. We had a ball in that noisy old car.

The first vehicle I actually owned was a cherry '47 Plymouth coupe that our local fifth grade teacher had traded for a '54 model. It took my entire summer wages, at a dollar an hour, to pay off the car dealer. A few other guys in school had cars too. There were a couple of '40 coupes, a '47 Ford Tudor, a '49 Chevy and a '50 Merc. These were pretty typical of what kids drove in the mid-50's. My Plymouth was a bit different to the standard Ford kids' stuff especially after my dad and I slipped a Chrysler Spitfire six under the hood.

The coupe became a hot rod with a milled head, dual carbs, chopped flywheel, a big clutch and a split exhaust manifold. I then fitted a set of Smittys for a cool sound. I had the hood louvered, then a bunch of coils were cut from the front springs to "Dago" it! Those were the days when you did mostly everything yourself because money was scarce. Living on a farm was a big plus because working with tools was a necessity.

We weren't experts, of course. The time dad and I decided to shave off the trunk handle on the '47, we warped the deck so bad I think we used about two tons of lead in an attempt to hide the damage. When it came time to paint the car at Rickman's Body Shop we got the bad news, "You need a new deck lid!"

Craig, my brother, and I farmed our own cornfield across the road from our house. We started out when we were about 10 years-old growing an acre of corn and then selling it just like this from the side of the road. Craig and I got a '41 Chevy two-door which we used to fill up with corn so we could truck it to grocery and fruit stores about the area, selling several dozen ears at a time.

About that time I remember dad picking up a '40 Ford truck with an Olds motor. He snaked the motor out of the pickup and we bolted it into a boat that we'd built in the barn behind the house. After that came a '49 Fordillac that I picked up in Visalia because we wanted its hot-rodded Caddy motor for the '40 Ford. My buddy, Jimmy White, wanted the goodies off the Cad' motor for his Caddy-powered, jet black '37 Chevy coupe so the '49 Ford got hauled to tin heaven, the local junk yard. I've no idea what became of the '40 pickup. Maybe it's a street rod today.

Jimmy quit school before graduating and

went to work for a Chevrolet dealer in Visalia. H.L. Shahan was the service manager at the time and his wife, Shirley Shahan, became a famous Super Stock - AF/X lady drag racer. Looking back, our part of the San Joaquin Valley has certainly produced many hot rods, customs, drag racers and circle track drivers!

Jimmy's Cad-powered Chevy, with my speed equipment stuff bolted in or on it, was a great hot street/drag car. One Sunday, we beat the Surabian Brothers' full race 302 GMC-powered '47 Chevy at the Dinuba Airport Drags. We turned 103 mph and thought we were the baddest drag racers around, deciding then and there to go down to Bakersfield and kick some butt.

Picture this—we're decked out in our gold striped white pith helmet racing uniforms, we're cool and pumped up—until we find out our first race is against Doug Cook's black '37 Chevy Howard Cams Special coupe. Our knees shook,

Above Left: Marilyn Jones' 8th Grade portrait. She went to Windsor Elementary School which had 11 girls and two boys in her class. When I met her a few years later, we were both going to school in Reedley. Dig those bangs!

Right: Dad always had the camera out shooting photos of the family. We were just on our way to church with grandma. That's Craig on the left and me on the right.

we were scared to death. We stuffed a bunch of rags in the carbs, like all the hot dog racers did, and pushed the car up through the staging lanes. Then, when they told us to fire it up we were so rattled we forgot to pull out the rags so the car wouldn't start. While this Dinuba fire drill was going on, Doug Cook was already down through the quarter at about 110 mph. We might have been the hottest dogs in Dinuba but at Bakersfield, we were just a couple of warm puppies.

In those days almost every town had a drag strip. The Vapor Trailers ran the Visalia Airport deal and we also raced at Madera. In 1957 they ran a two-way championship which raced the cars down the drag strip and then ran them back.

In 1959, it was a major happening to attend the biggest deal of all—The Bakersfield Fuel and Gas Championships—which history has shown to be one of drag racing's most famous events.

I became known as the Dinuba Kid and I always had one of the lowest cars around. I mean l-o-o-w. My buddy, Tommy Jackson, and I earned the local reputation of "the people to see if you want to get low."

On the farm we had a huge chain hoist and cutting torches. We'd whack coils and make a few bucks. I remember once after school we did three cars before dinner. At first we did it the hard way, lowered the A arms, removed the coils, cut them, and bolted everything back together. This took a long time but eventually we figured out that if we jerked the car up in the air with the chain hoist and let the wheels hang down, we could torch away, popping out the unwanted sections of coils with a rusty crowbar. It was dirty, nasty, work but—somebody had to do it!

Almost 30 years later, after our house had burned down (not our fault) and the property owners had demolished the barn, they wondered about the four-foot high mound of spring sections and pieces of coils lying all over the place.

Remembering back, Tommy and I must have slammed a hundred cars. Billy Umeda's '52 Merc hardtop was a bone crusher after we got through with it, so was Ronnie Bathhouser's '55 Buick Century. Ray Mitchum's '40 Ford got the long shackle treatment. He and his buddy, Garland Sharp, flipped it one day when it swayed out of control but nobody got hurt. Johnny Jesperson put small tires on the front of his '50 Olds that we had lowered, and when he blew one of the tires the bottom A-arm dug into the road and flipped him and the car into a vineyard.

That was a clincher for the Highway Patrol! They started coming after us for being too low and I got my first ticket for my slammed Plymouth. With 500 X 15's and no rubber snubbers in the front and 820 X 15's on the rear, the car had a serious stance. The cop took a picture from under the rear of the car towards the front, just to prove his case. It was a grim moment. I was so young my mom had to accompany me to court. Aside from that encounter with the law, the cops were cool. I guess they figured most of this stuff was just innocent fun.

It wasn't until I graduated from high school that I had the Plymouth really looking good. I got a job for $1.25 an hour at the local lumber yard which enabled me to buy a set of Moon discs, a set of wide whitewalls, a fresh bright yellow paint job and a white interior with silver welting.

Later, a guy named Vance came up from Ventura and, in our dirt-floored barn, painted the purple scallops. He also blew a beautiful set of flames on Garland Sharps' '40 Ford. I'll never forget Garland. After his car was finally flamed and finished he seemed to run out of something to do. He told me: "Gary, my hot rod is finished and my dresser drawer's full of new T-shirts and that's just about as good as life can ever get. So, I think I'll just up and join the Navy." And he did! That's the way things were for some guys back in the 50's.

I still had plenty to do because cruising had become my life; fixing up cars and dragging the main streets in Visalia, Dinuba, Reedley, and

Below: The day I got the Plymouth was December, 18th 1954. I wheeled that machine into the parking lot at Dinuba High like I owned the place. I purchased the car for $400 from the local Chrysler dealer who had traded it from a local school teacher. I was 15 years-old and, as you can tell, it's winter, the girls are wearing top coats and a touch of fog is hanging in the background. That's my high school pal, Don Troxel, staring at the camera

Above: I started working the Plymouth over with a set of whitewalls, Moon hubcaps and red rims but that didn't quite do it for me; I had visions of a really low machine. After this photo was taken, Craig and I took the Plymouth into the barn, jacked it up and sliced out a couple of coils up front. I dropped it off the jack and the coupe hit the stoppers. Suddenly, it dawned on us that we had cut too much but, oh boy, did it look great down in the weeds.

Below: The Plymouth went into black primer for a while but then I settled on Ford Sunflower Yellow as my color choice. We nosed the hood and decked the trunk lid before I had Rickman in Dinuba paint the car. To finance the Plymouth I worked every summer for my dad. Craig and I would get up at 5 a.m., drive out to one of the acreages that my dad rented, and plow all day. Dad would drive me to the land, gas up my tractor and leave me to dig ditches or cultivate the crop, dropping off my brother at another tractor to do the same thing. He would come back at noon to feed us and then pick us up in the evening.

Right: The scallops on the nose of the Plymouth were applied by Vance from Ventura. They ran around the hood and the front fenders and down along the side. They also flashed back over the roof. I also painted everything underneath white including the fender wells, firewall and the engine. By this stage we had learned how to lower the cars without having them hit the stoppers! The Plymouth was lowered here with about one and half coils cut out up front and 3-inch lowering blocks in the rear.

Fresno, kept my spare time totally occupied. I was no high school jock because I wasn't big enough for the school sports. After some JV stuff with basketball and baseball I figured I wasn't the Letter Sweater type. About all I lived for was going downtown in my '47 every night.

I was lucky, too, because we had a large gasoline tank on the farm and I could gas up anytime I needed. The gasoline and charging car repair parts to the farm account were probably the only times we were glad our folks had farms.

Cruising Visalia was cool because it was a large town—but Fresno was the place, a big city with Stan's Drive-in. Many kinds of cars would show up and Fresno must have had the lowest cars in the world.

Reedley was a neat place to hang out, too. In the summer the girls would be hired by the fruit packing plants located downtown and when they got off work we'd see them for a soda or cruise Main Street. They'd also go out to Reedley Beach for swimming parties where the hot deal was to leap off the bridge with an inner tube and float down the river to the next bridge, all the while nursing on a six pack, then hitch a

Left: Marilyn was a senior in high school about this time and, like all kids in a small country town, we had our hangouts; Reedley Beach on the Kings River was one of our favorites during the summer.

Right: That's us at the Fresno County Fair in 1958, messing about in the photo booth.

Above: You can see that the coupe was getting lower from this angle. It also shows the roof scallop. When we first started lowering other guys' cars it used to take us an hour and half. Then we got wise and started jacking up the cars and knocking the cut coil out with a pry bar as we sliced them up. When we moved out of the shop on the farm and they pulled down the old barn, the owner complained about the huge mound of coil springs hidden in the weeds!

ride with a buddy back to the bridge and do it all over again. We had some hell-raising parties out at our farm, too - when my folks went away on a fishing trip down the Klamath River.

Soon, however, "growing up" with its realities and responsibilities began to take over the simple party 'n' fun and cruising of the 50's. As that fantastic decade of four wheel diversions drew to a close, our lives began to change in many ways. Our style of custom cruising and rodding fun with older cars disappeared, like someone had flicked off the lights.

Dad gave up farming and took over the management of a new bowling alley in Dinuba and in 1961 Marilyn and I were married. I remember we went bowling on our honeymoon.

I can't help thinking how lucky I was, to be the right age at exactly the right time to actually be there, enjoying the best of early custom cruising and rodding fun. Lucky, too, that my father and family had understood and tolerated all my cruising craziness. A new generation was taking over the streets but the cars they were driving and what they were doing with them wasn't exciting to me. I certainly didn't lose my love for cars but I couldn't know it would be another decade before I'd find myself behind the wheel of a street rod again.

# Marilyn's Story

In the fifties, my home town of Reedley, California, was not unlike hundreds of heartland towns; our lifestyles were all similar, and the only difference, really, was in the crops we grew. I was a share-cropper's daughter, one of five children growing up in a rented house with dad the bread winner working on the farmland to support the family. How hard we worked as a team on the farm just to make ends meet! We'd work all summer and earn enough to buy our school clothes. Then mom would take us shopping just before school started. Believe me, buying new clothes was a giant step up from mom's sewing!

Reedley was basically a Mennonite community. They may have been the salt of the earth, but there was little in the way of fun and

Above: Marilyn used this '55 Lincoln Capri two-door hardtop to commute to Fresno where she worked at Brownie Muffler. I bought the Capri after I sold the Plymouth. I really wanted a '55 Chevy but couldn't afford it. Originally, I wasn't going to do anything to it but after a couple of months I got the urge to lower it so I chopped a coil and a half up front, then fitted 2.1/2-inch blocks in the rear. I also changed the 8.00's on the front for 6.40's. It was a great machine; you could drive it fast as you wanted.

games in their lives. I remember when I taught my little Mennonite friend, Shirley, to play Old Maid, she told her mom that I'd taught her to play cards and she was never allowed to come over and play again.

My first high school days were somewhat intimidating. Having attended only a small country school from kindergarten through eighth grade, I was moved into such a new environment that at first I couldn't even walk down the main hall because of all the boys lined up on both sides checking out the girls! It didn't take me long, though, to blend in and even become a social butterfly. High school was a wonderful experience and the friends I made I still see at some of our street rod and custom events.

This brings me to the subject of cars, you bet they were an integral part of my young life! Farm kids could drive at 14 and my dad would let me handle his old '40 Ford pickup with its huge, long gearshift lever, as well as the farm tractor. I learned to drive on that old tractor before I could even reach the pedals and, while tractor driving was actually work, it was also great fun, not unlike some of my later adventures in street rods.

Living outside town meant that a car was a necessity of life and in 1958 my father gave my twin sister Carolyn and I a cherry aqua-colored '49 Merc instead of cash for clothes.

Reedley High School shared some facilities and a cafeteria with Reedly College and, naturally, the college guys checked out the high school girls. One day my girlfriend Jan Ware and I were walking home from school when a super low, yellow '47 Plymouth coupe rolled up and stopped beside us. It was Gary and his friend Tommy Jackson who offered to give us a lift home. After considering our reputations and how this scene might look to this ultra conservative community—we promptly piled into Gary's car. High school girls riding around with a couple of college guys was a pretty daring move

Below: Our wedding day with both parents. My folks, Anne and Glen, are on the right and Marilyn's, Carl and Ludie Jones, are on the left. She looked fabulous and I'd just got a buzzed flattop for the occasion. We were married at my folks' place by my grandfather who was a Mennonite preacher.

in a small town in the middle fifties.

Gary was the ultimate cruiser and that suited me just fine. Places like Hutchinson's Drive-In or the Tren Biswell Ford parking lot in Dinuba were the places to be seen. "Dragging Main" had only recently become a national pastime and we took full advantage of every opportunity. Sometimes the guys would venture out to Canal Road for some street racing but as I recall it was no big deal and, best of all, nobody ever got hurt.

Gary and I were never alone on a date, there were always a couple of buddies along and his car, a down-in-the-weeds Plymouth, was so low it bottomed out on everything. Crossing a

set of railroad tracks was a bone-jarring experience. Eventually we started using my '49 Merc for smoother riding four wheeled fun.

After graduating from high school I tried college for a year, then got a job at Brownie Muffler in Fresno. Gary bought a '55 Lincoln hardtop then slammed it down to metal-to-metal contact. Just before Gary and I got married in 1961 he traded the Lincoln in for $300 on a new '61 Ford Tudor hardtop.

By then my dad was selling Fords at Tren Biswell so we got a close-out special. We financed a $2100 long-term commitment for $67.00 a month. Thirty days after we were married Gary had to serve his six month active

Below: Eventually we sold the Lincoln and purchased a '61 Ford Victoria Hard Top. This photo shows me and my buzz cut just home for the weekend from Fort Ord where I was serving in the California Army National Guard for six months.

Above: This photo was taken after the "Sacramento Mile" at the State Fairgrounds in Sacramento which is now called Cal Expo. J.C. Agajanian promoted the event on the mile dirt track and it always attracted some of the best drivers, including a young Mario Andretti seen here with Marilyn and her girlfriends, Bonnie and Janice.

Right: Gary Bettenhausen was another driver we liked to see race at Sacramento. Over the years we met a lot of these drivers and had a great time at the races. That's my old buddy Johnny O'Loan on the left with me on the right in the Goodyear jacket.

duty with the California National Guard and earned the monumental sum of $56.00 a month. I was footing the bills for food, rent and survival out of my muffler shop earnings.

In the meantime, we fell behind on the car payments so the finance company came to talk to us. This was absolutely humiliating and the lesson learned was that we'd never, ever, buy another new car. We'd never again make car payments; if we couldn't pay cash for a car, we figured we couldn't afford it!

Gary settled down and went to work for Western Homes who built houses in the Central Valley. It was a big outfit and he spent three years with them before joining Gillette, the razor company.

Gary's first company car was a '64 Chevy four-door and we went everywhere in it - boat races, sprint and dirt track car races, Bakersfield Drags, Clovis Raceway - if something raced, went fast and made a noise, we attended.

We were living in Fresno when Marty, our first son, was born and trans-ferred to Fremont, 30 miles east of of San Francisco, when our second son, Marc, entered the world. Gary had a good job but in order to enjoy everything that life, cars, and water sports had to offer, I got a job packaging meat products.

I usually had to work on Saturdays so Gary would take the boys to the waterways to ski behind our boat called the "River Roadster." I'd join them after I got off work. Looking back, having fun was a lot of work!

We've always had a great time with our various cars, from our lowered rides of the 50's, our T-Bucket in the 60's, to our old 70's Deuce Tudor which remains the signature car of the Goodguys.

In 1977 the four of us headed to St. Paul, destined for the Street Rod Nats. We headed

Above: It may be hard to believe but I used to wear a tie to work every day when I worked for Western Homes as a cost accountant. I certainly learned how to run a project working there and that gave me a great grounding in financial management.

north through Seattle, then onto the Canadian Nationals through Banff, and into Winnipeg, ultimately arriving in Minnesota. We lived in the '32, sleeping in shifts for what seemed like weeks. Those were the pioneering days of street rodding and there was a thrill and an excitement to a cross country trip; no place was too far to drive. These adventures still continue to this day as our street rods remain a driving force for Gary, for me, and for the Goodguys.

Above: Eventually we repainted the '61 Ford Victoria dark green and had it re-upholstered. Marilyn drove it to work as by now I had a company car with my job at Carter Products. This was taken about 1968 with Marc kicking about in his cowboy boots.

Right: I had a neighbor, who worked at the local Ford dealership, rebuild this 390 for the '61 Ford. He installed a mild cam and a bunch of other trick Ford Performance stuff. It didn't run a diddle but it sure looked good.

We became involved in quarter midget racing with the Hayward Club when Marty got interested in cars and raced a couple of seasons with this little car. Back in those days you had to create almost everything yourself and that included the driver's suit which my grandma had made for Marty.

# GARY'S SCRAPBOOK

I started taking photos at the events we attended and really enjoyed that part of the trip. I liked to get into the pits and shoot photos of what was happening. My photos, and my friendship with Bruce Olson, eventually led me to shooting photos and writing stories for several magazines including *Rod Action, Hot Rod* and *Rod and Custom*. The photos here were taken in the fifties and early sixties at events from Bakersfield to Fremont.

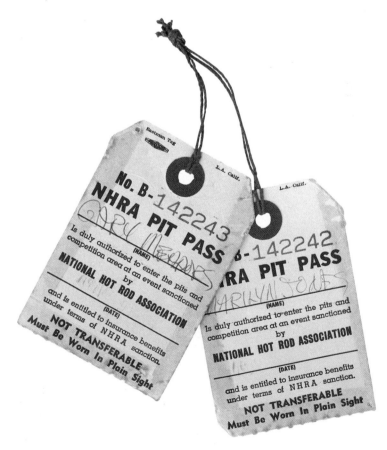

Romeo Palamides raced at the events we attended. I caught the car in the staging lanes at Bakersfield while the crew waited their turn and for Romeo to arrive. This was a cool looking dragster with its short wheel base, all aluminum body and an injected Hemi. Romeo built this dragster and had Pete Ogden drive it for him. Romeo went on to build many kinds of drag racing machinery and invented an array of performance parts including 12-spoke aluminum wheels for dragsters.

Left: In 1958, Howard Johansen's blown twin-engined monster was wildly exciting to see in action and incredibly noisy when it was. That's Howard working on the car in the middle. He was always the one "to push the envelope" and his wooden bodywork gave him the honor of owning "the World's Fastest Plywood."

Below: Johansen's twin-engined rail evolved somewhat with aluminum replacing the plywood bodywork and fuel injection replacing the Strombergs.

Above: Another wild piece of engineering was the sidewinder dragster owned by Chuck Jones and raced by Joe Mailliard Automotive Engineering. Powered by a cross-mounted blown Hemi, the dragster was driven by Jack Chrisman. In this photo you can see the huge twin chain drive which drove a straight axle to both rear wheels.

This classic early dragster, with a drilled front axle, Moon discs and custom aluminum body, was owned by Ernie Hashim, Howard Hylton and Bill Crossley. Ernie was the local M&H tire dealer in Bakersfield and is still the West Coast distributor. It featured a front mounted Potvin-style GMC supercharger and Hilborn fuel injection. I recall the car ran pretty well at this Bakersfield event with a top speed somewhere close to 175 mph. The car was in the Smokers Club and was driven by Bill Crossley. I shot this at the first Fuel and Gas Championships in 1959 in Bakersfield, California.

Above: At some Vapor Trailers events at Visalia Airport you would see show rods being drag raced. I liked the white interior on this five-window with its unusual tuck and roll floor and door panels. This was a sweet looking car from every angle and ran B/Gas.

Below: This photo of the Dago Special is from the mid-fifties at Visalia, typical of the roadsters which raced in these small drag racing events. It was unusual at that time for a race car be painted in turquoise green but it sure looked smart.

Above: The Ventura Motor Monarchs raced a couple of wild machines over the years including this Competition Coupe powered by a blown Chrysler Hemi. It was built with home-engineering talent including a custom blower drive, adapter kit and induction. The chopped roof was filled with a section of sheet metal.

Below: Known as the Giant Killer, the "Waters, Sughrue and Guinn" modified roadster ran a blown DeSoto. At the first Fuel and Gas Championships it raced in a 350-car field against all comers losing out to Art Chrisman's Hustler in the final round. The final round was run in near darkness but Tony Waters still turned 174.41 mph at 9.41.

Above: Jocko's Porting Service Streamliner was also at
Bakersfield for the Fuel and Gas Championships in 1959.
This was the first time Jocko ran it with a supercharged
engine topped with eight "floatless" 48 Stromberg carbure-
tors. Jazzy Nelson was the driver of this streamliner which
Jocko had designed using the first advanced aerodynam-
ics for drag racing. Its best run was at Riverside with a
178.21 mph/8.35 second ET which set the world ET record
at the time, beating Chrisman's Hustler record of 8.45
seconds.

Below: The Hustler has been through more transformations than most street rods. It is seen here in March 1959, fitted with new, raw aluminum bodywork surrounding a fresh blown Chrysler. With Art Chrisman at the wheel, the Hustler was Top Eliminator at the Bakersfield meet where Jim Deist and Art first experimented with a parachute.

Above: Another of the Ventura Motor Monarchs' race cars was the altered B/Fuel Fiat Topolino coupe run by Clarkson and Klocke. This cool looking little machine featured Moon discs and an Ardun flathead. The other Motor Monarchs' coupe can be seen just behind the Fiat.

Right: I have seen some strange setups over the years but the Palmquist and Weeks fuel roadster had to be one of the wildest, with its 10 Strombergs mounted on a manifold attached to a front-mounted super-charger. It must have been a nightmare to tune with that Hemi sitting amidships and enough plumbing to feed a small apartment!

Below: Art Arfons toured all over the country for years. I first caught up with his "Green Monster XI" at Bakersfield in the sixties when it was powered by a huge Allison V12 aero engine. It was a crudely built machine but it impressed everyone who saw it.

UNITED STATES
FUEL & GAS
CHAMPIONSHIPS

PRESENTED BY:

SMOKERS INC.
BAKERSFIELD, CALIF.

ADMISSION $6.00

GLOBE TICKET COMPANY, PHILA.

Souvenir-Retain This Coupon

05273

Above: The Panella Brothers from Stockton, California, have been involved with hot rods and drag racing for years. Their slick '40 Willys pickup was always beautifully prepared. Powered by a blown Chevy, the Willys was a consistent class winner.

Below: The first Sears Point drag meet was very popular. The track was new and ran up hill which necessitated some adjustments in driving style. Many top fuel racers turned out for this event including Don Garlits who arrived with his "Wynnscharger" Top Fuel car. It was decked out in a new paint scheme and Don can be seen pushing the machine back to the pits.

Above: Chuck Flores' "Sour Sister" dragster looked very
much like Ed Roth's Yellow Fang with its pointed vertical
wing at the rear. This classic early seventies dragster is
seen here at Fremont with Marty checking it out.

Below: Guasco's "Pure Hell" Fuel Altered was one of the most famous race cars from the seventies. This wild car and wild driver put on some of the most spectacular drag racing ever seen at Fremont. Powered by an iron-blocked Hemi topped with a blower and fuel injection, it emanated brute horsepower just sitting still. With Dale "The Snail" Emery at the wheel this machine turned 7.27 at 221.41 mph. The car was later badly damaged in a towing accident but has recently been restored and is now on display at the NHRA museum in LaVerne, California. A slightly longer replica is now raced on the nostalgia drag racing circuit.

This is my favorite photo from the November, 1966, meet at Lions Drag Strip with Jim Davis riding in his Top Fuel dragster during the push-down for the opening of the evening event. Dig that Pontiac Wagon!

# Hot Rodding Around

Street rodding never died, it just took a brief rest while muscle cars were the fad. The old car rodding revivals took place during the late 60's; the T-Bucket roadster was the big thing. By this time I was established, so to speak, and had invested in a semi-finished Andy's Instant T. As luck would have it, I met an old friend from Dinuba who was also building one of Andy's T's. At the time I was selling Carter Wallace Products (like Little Liver Pills and Arrid Extra Dry) and Art Branam, an ex-Dinuba guy, was managing a Gemco store in the San Francisco Bay Area. It was a reunion, comparing notes, and bench racing. This chance meeting convinced me that the kind of rodding I'd always enjoyed was on its way back. I was a family man by then with two sons so when the T was finished we all climbed on board.

It was a dependable little car, with it's 318 "Plymouth" motor that never failed to start. We never hesitated to pack up the family (four in a T-bucket—a sight to behold) and head for the race tracks in Calistoga or Sacramento. I even raced the little jewel at Fremont Drag Strip, just a stone's throw from our home, where it ran over 100 in the quarter. We were sprint car race fanatics and everywhere we went to the roundy-round tracks we were known as "those guys in the T-bucket." Our T was nothing very special, we knew it, but it didn't matter—we attended every car show, indoor and out, that we could find.

Although there were a few great old-time car clubs that had weathered the declining

Right: Marilyn, Marty and Marc at Andy's Picnic in Crow Canyon Park with the Beer-T. This was the second year we went to the picnic in the rod. For its first outing we drove it without any interior, but this photo shows the car complete.

interest in cars between 1960 and 1970 and hosted their own private runs, rod runs weren't really happening yet. Indoor displays in shopping malls and parking lots were "where it was at" for most of us.

We met many great people during the early 70's who were in the same bucket with the rest of us. Some had old 50's and 60's Deuce and Model A hot rods and many of us had fresh T's. We had cars, wanted to drive them but, really,

a 100 mile trip to the Gold Country in the foothills of the Sierra Mountains. Picture a long caravan of hot rods, parts falling off, running out of gas, flat tires, and stopping constantly at filling stations because someone had to go to the bathroom. And how often did those tiny T bucket beer keg gas tanks run dry! It must have taken over four hours to go a hundred miles but the frustrations of group gangs and rod caravans are now only fond memories.

had no place to go.

However, rodding was slowly re-emerging and clubs were forming. Ed and Mary Lee, Bruce and Dorothy Olson, Dino and Joyce Ramacciotti, Jim and Pat Gomes were a few of the people who were instrumental in the creation of the Nor-Cal Early Iron Car Club. Sixty to 70 people would attend a club meeting. We'd have little rod runs (we didn't call them runs at the time) at public parks close by, and once we took

Above: The Oakland Roadster Show used the Beer-T for this promotional photo for the '69 event. It was in its first generation here, finished in Riviera Gray. Back then we just put our car in the show for the heck of it.

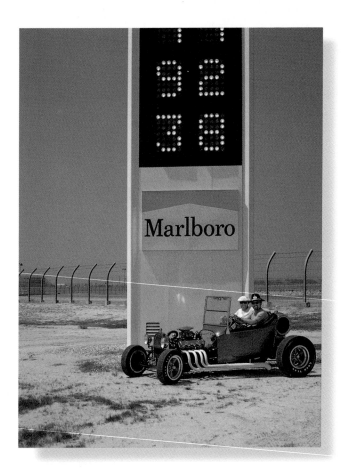

Right: In late 1971, I had Tony Del Rio paint the Beer-T pearl yellow. I added a scoop to the engine, new headlight stands, headers, a wooden dash and even wider Goodyear tires on the rear. We showed the T at several shows and eventually sold the car at the Oakland show in 1972.

like me finds himself on a smooth asphalt race track in a hot rod, temptation over-rides intelligence. I floor-boarded the roadster. Before we entered the first turn somebody was on to us and they chased us down in a Plymouth Super Bee, escorting us right out of the place. Fun? You bet!

We sold the T at the Oakland Roadster Show to a guy who wanted it badly. Having been taken for a short blast along the freeway, he plunked down the cash right on the spot. A month later I heard about a Deuce Tudor up in Paradise, a little town near Chico, in Northern California. We drove a couple hundred miles up there and found a sorry looking brown '32 with gold flames and gold velour upholstery. It sat low with its Corvair front end, some kind of coil sprung Pontiac rear end, and a problem with the lug nuts. On impulse and lust I shelled out a whopping $2,500 for the '32 and we headed home.

We almost made it, too, but the alternator stopped charging, the left rear wheel came loose and the brakes went out - quite a contrast to the dependable roadster we'd driven far and wide. When we got home the '32 sat rejected and was hardly used until one day my friends and I decided to fix it up. The Corvair front end needed serious attention and we knew the big club of a rear end had to go. Unfortunately, its

Above: We drove the "Beer T" down to the Ontario Motor Speedway for the very first Indy Car race. This photo, shot at the base of the timing tower, was taken the day before the race. Right after we took it we set off around the track and nearly made it one time before we were diverted out the gate by security who told us to "just keep on going."

To this day, I can't figure out why guys trailer their cars. Twenty-five years ago, we took off with no spare tire, no tools, a seven gallon gas tank, and a car full of little kids. We worried about nothing - it was an adventure!

In 1970 my buddy Pete Choquette and I blasted down to L.A. in the T bucket to see a midget race and the very first race at the Ontario Motor Speedway. I knew a fellow, Phil Casey, from Fresno who was crew chief for Gearhart Racers so we got into the pit area. The day before the race we found a driveway that led onto the track. I thought we'd take some pictures of the "T" on the track. However, when a guy

Right: The "Beer-T" was built from an Andy's Instant T kit in the late 60's and early 70's, powered by a 318 cubic inch Plymouth and rolled on five-spoke Americans. This photo was taken after it had been finished with a Tony Del Rio yellow paint job, gold lettering across the cowl, and a chromed firewall.

Above: Touring on a cold winter's day with the Nor-Cal Early Iron. This is Burnham and his wife in his '23 roadster which was stretched to look like a tub. Nice outfits, eh?. Burnham looks like he's set to rob a convenience store. Photo: Bruce Olson.

new 9-inch Ford rear end was installed by a drag racer who had used a set of lightweight ladder bars and a super soft set of rear springs.

As soon as he had finished the rear end we headed for the Street Rod Nationals in Tulsa, Oklahoma. Larry Westervelt and his wife Lani in their '32 Vicky went with us. We made it there in fine shape and had a great time participating in most of the driving events, and when we entered the Streetkhana we decided to do it "California style"—four people in the car for a down-in-the-dirt, evil, low look. Unfortunately, we were down-in-the-dirt a little too much. I tried to dirt-track the sedan and slide around the cones which resulted in the rear end being ripped right out from under the car!

At the conclusion of the trip home, the most important chapter of my life began.

Above: The '32 after it was fitted with Buick Skylark wire wheels. The Tudor is seen here at Mission San Jose looking just as it did before we moved to Tennessee. This was the last of the brown cars.

Right: We drove the '32 to the Street Rod Nationals in Tulsa, Oklahoma, in 1973. In those days there were a variety of events and I used to run the Streetkhana. However, at Tulsa I snapped the ladder bars right off the rear end so we had to make repairs at the event. The first guy who welded it worked in a lawn mower shop. He said, "I don't know too much about welding but I guess I can fix it!" It broke again on the way home in Arizona so the next time I had it welded up by a pro.

Left: After we were transferred to Germantown, Tennessee, by Carter/Wallace Products, I tore the '32 down completely. We sandblasted the frame and body, changed the front end around, and started on a complete ground-up rebuild.

Below: I did a story for *Rod Action* on installing a station wagon roof top into the '32. I discovered that a '62 Ford station wagon roof had just the right bow to it after my buddy, who was doing the same thing to a '32 four-door Cadillac, had used a '64 wagon roof panel. He had cut both years to see which would suit his job and the '64 worked fine in his conversion, so he gave me the '62.

Above: The new chassis with the Chevy 350, Powerglide, and Buick Skylark wheels, a 9-inch Ford with ladder bars and Firebird disc brakes.

Right: By this time I had completed magazine "How To" articles for *Rod Action* on filling the top, putting in the glass, installing a 350 Chevy with a Powerglide while rebuilding the '32. When it came to putting the body back on the chassis I needed lots of extra hands.

Above: Just before this Memphis Street Rods
event, I learned that Carter/Wallace Products
had decided to move us back to California. I
was one of the organizers and motivators of this
club event so I was involved with everything and
everyone. At the end of the event, I got called
up on stage for a special presentation. I figured
they were going to give me a jacket or plaque or
something special. They brought out a box and
I was thinking "great." The next thing, I get a pie
in the face, for going back to California. Oh well,
it was a great time, and a gift I will always
remember.

Below: I took this group shot of the Nor-Cal Early Iron Hot Rod Club at Livermore after participating in a Saturday parade. As you can see, the club had flourished with a great group of T-buckets and rods.

"STREET IS NEAT"

Right: This was the flyer for the "First Lodi West Coast Street Rod Mini Nationals" in 1973 with the Nor-Cal Early Iron club. The Nor-Cal Early Iron Club was started by me, Burnham, Jim Gomes, Bruce Olson, Ed Lee and some others. It grew to a good size and I wrote to Dick Wells, president of the NSRA, to see if we could organize a sanctioned event. Larry Westervelt (who now works for Goodguys), Jim, and I found the fairgrounds in Lodi. We rented the place and ran the event as the West Coast Mini-Nationals in 1973. We created a program for this event, my brother Craig designed it and I sold the ads. It was quite a deal - 566 hot rods turned up from as far away as British Columbia, Arizona, and Southern California.

Left: We were using "Street is Neat" years ago!

Below: This photo is from Winston-Salem, North Carolina, just after we arrived at the Nats-South event in 1979. Bob Reynolds, Jim Ewing and I looked like a bunch of bearded wild men from the West Coast.

# SPECTATORS WELCOME

## Adults $2.00          Children $1.00

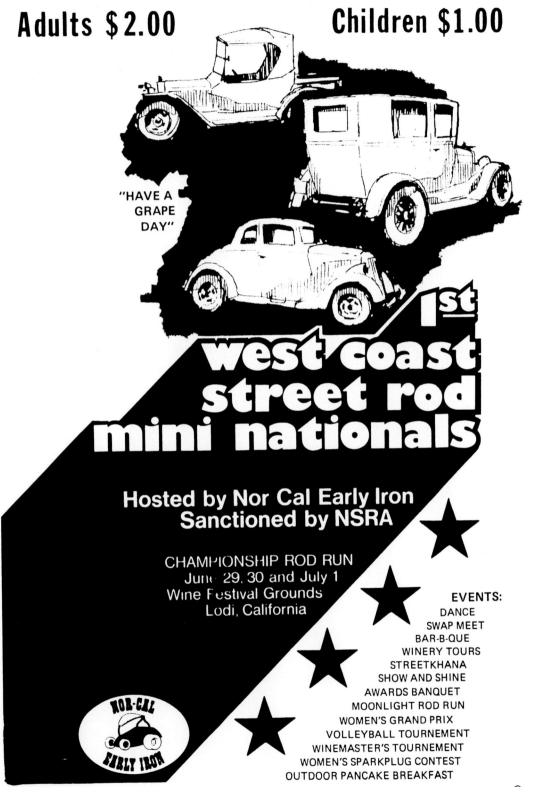

"HAVE A GRAPE DAY"

# 1st
# west coast
# street rod
# mini nationals

## Hosted by Nor Cal Early Iron
## Sanctioned by NSRA

CHAMPIONSHIP ROD RUN
June 29, 30 and July 1
Wine Festival Grounds
Lodi, California

EVENTS:
DANCE
SWAP MEET
BAR-B-QUE
WINERY TOURS
STREETKHANA
SHOW AND SHINE
AWARDS BANQUET
MOONLIGHT ROD RUN
WOMEN'S GRAND PRIX
VOLLEYBALL TOURNEMENT
WINEMASTER'S TOURNEMENT
WOMEN'S SPARKPLUG CONTEST
OUTDOOR PANCAKE BREAKFAST

NOR-CAL EARLY IRON

Above: Marilyn and I, on the right, pose with Bruce and Dorothy Olson for a publicity photo for the San Jose Street Rod event. Bruce's chopped and channeled five-window 392 Hemi-powered '32 is seen here with my '32. I was event director and Bruce was the event coordinator.

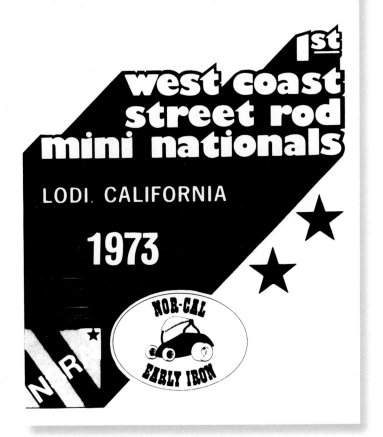

# V.I.P. PASS

## 1st west coast street rod mini nationals

### LODI, CALIFORNIA

### 1973

NOR-CAL EARLY IRON

Below: Our creeper racers developed some wild machines so we organized a lot of racing at the events including the Western Street Rod Mini Nationals in Merced, California. This group of about 10 teams created parking lot excitement as they screamed around the tracks we set up.

In 1980 I created the first Mini Nationals in Ventura, California. It took some work to get it organized but we had a great time. I drove down in the '32 popping off this photo at the end of the show.

**As told by Bill Burnham**

# The whole darned thing started, simply enough, way back in 1978 . . .

Tommy Walsh, ex-professional drag racer, had just finished a fully equipped, extra large shop next to his home in which to pursue his latest hot-set-up auto sport and hobby, Street (hot) Rodding. Barely a few blocks away in the little town of Danville, California, lived a couple of unusual hot rod dudes who were deep into having fun with cars.

One was the ultimate organizer, Gary Meadors, later to become the Goodguy himself. The other was the irreverent and opinionated Bill Burnham, who also later would view rodding through only his eyes on the pages of several prominent magazines.

These three fellows had three things in common: Their love of hot rods dating back to the middle 1950's, their penchant for "party

Above: The first infamous Danville Dukes bus trip to LA. We organized this bus trip for 40 to 50 guys to an ISCA car show at the Anaheim Convention Center in 1979. Bill Burnham, Tommy Walsh, and I, rented a ballroom at the convention center and did our own Academy of Hot Rodding Awards, presenting dinky 3-inch high trophies. It was a lot of fun and I don't think anyone came home sober.

# VALLEY LOADERS

CONSTITUTION AND By Laws OF The VALLEY LOADERS Rod Club.

PURPOSE AND DIRECTION OF ~~THIS CLUB~~ The VALLEY LOADERS
    A. ENJOYMENT of Street Rodding WITH A MINIMUM
        OF ENCUMBERANCES.
    B. CAPITALIZE ON The ORGANIZATIONS OF OTHERS.

QUALIFICATIONS FOR MEMBERSHIP. *LICENSED OR NON LICENSED.* *~~REGISTERED OR NON REGISTERED AND LICENSED.~~*
    A. OWNERSHIP OF ONE OR MORE, PRE 1949 VEHICLE.
    B. ~~BE A~~ A MEMBER OF This CLUB MUST CURRENTLY
hold, have held, or CONTEMPLATES APPLICATION FOR A
~~CALIFORNIA~~ *STATE* DRIVERS ~~LICENSE~~ LICENSE.
    C. MUST AGREE TO STRICTLY ABIDE BY The
~~FOLLOWING~~ BY LAWS MENTIONED HEREIN.

### By LAWS.
The ~~FOLLOWING~~ by-Laws shall be CONSIDERED AS
"ABSOLUTE" AND UN-AMMENDABLE UNLESS A MEMBER ~~CONSIDERS~~ *FEELS* THAT
A PARTICULAR SEGMENT ~~TOO~~ RESTRICTIVE. In Such an EVENT
The member or MEMBERS CAN CONSIDER The OFFENDING
By-LAW AS NON EXISTANT.

### CLUB MEETINGS.
    A. A CLUB MEETING SHALL BE DEEMED IN SESSION *AS OFFICIALLY*
when ~~TWO~~ Two or MORE MEMBERS find themselves ENGAGED
IN CONVERSATION CONCERNING STREET Rods. (Telephone CONVERSATIONS *INCLUDED.*
    B. CLUB MEMBERS should attempt TO ATTEND
OR ENGAGE Themselves IN NO LESS than ONE MEETING PER YEAR.
    C. No ATTEMPT SHALL BE made to formally ~~request~~
the ~~ATTENDANCE~~ *ASSEMBLY* OF The entire MEMBERSHIP for A MEETING or
ANY OTHER FUNCTION. Such a request will be CONSIDERED AS
BAD TASTE.

(OVER)

CLUB OFFICERS.

A. ALL MEMBERS OF THIS CLUB shall hold the TITLE OF "CLUB PRESIDENT". ALL WIVES AND GIRL FRIENDS SHALL BE CONSIDERED AS VICE PRESIDENTS.

MEMBERSHIP LIMITATIONS.

A. There SHALL BE NO LESS THAN TWO MEMBERS. SHOULD the OFFICAL CLUB ROSTER FALL BELOW TWO, QUALIFIED MALE MEMBERS, the club will be CONSIDERED DISBANDED

DUES AND FINES.

A. There shall be NO CLUB DUES

B. FINES Appropriate for the OFFENCE shall be LEVIED AT The DISCRETION OF THE CLUB PRESIDENT. NOTE: PRESIDENTS AND VICE PRESIDENTS ARE EXEMPT FROM ANY FORM OF FINE, JUDGEMENT, OR CENSURE.

CLUB UNIFORM.

A. The OFFICAL CLUB UNIFORM SHALL BE MEET The following description.

1. ANY GARMENT OR COMBINATION OF GARMENTS That ADEQUATELY COVER The BODY's "PRIVATE PARTS"

2. UPPER GARMENTS ARE "OPTIONAL" FOR VICE PRESIDENTS.

3. LEVIS AND MANUFACTURER'S TEE shirts ARE PREFERRED APPEAL.

B ANY ATTEMPT TO EMULATE OTHER ORGANIZATIONS WITH SUCH APPEAL AS CLUB JACKETS, TEE SHIRTS ETC. SHALL BE CONSIDERED AS IN POOR TASTE.

time," and their previous membership in the same typical (1970's) active and highly respected California street rod club.

The three put their heads together and decided to have a garage warming party, for guys only. While planning the party an idea emerged to create a Phantom Car Club. With a good measure of disrespect for the typical car club status quo the irascible trio dreamed up the "Danville Dukes." They figured their club would be a one-night stand only and then would become instantly forgotten. With this in mind they purchased three tattered saffron (yellow) tuxedos as club uniforms and set down in print the constitution and by-laws of the Danville Dukes car club.

Essentially, there would be NO rules! NO dues, NO roll call, NO new and old business, NO minutes of the meeting. There would also be NO wives and NO girlfriends. Every member would be a club president. Each new member would be admitted free but would have to pay $5,000 to get out of the club. If anyone attended a Dukes' club function he would automatically become a member.

This car club counter-culture deal was to be a time when, and a place where, even the most hard-core clubber could kick back, have fun and chuckle a bit about rules, club colors, and regulation-sanctioned runs. On the night of their party someone suggested that the Danville Dukes might well be the first Unclub Car Club in the U.S.

Previous Two Pages: This is a copy of the original statement of purpose for the Danville Dukes which at the time Bill Burnham had named the "Valley Loaders." According to Bill, the idea for the club was "a hopelessly unorthodox, unstructured, free-loading, UN-CLUB" . . . hence the "Loaders" nametag. It was specifically aimed at attracting guys who had already suffered through years of rinky-dink car club B-S."

A group of the Dukes helped me stage this photo for a magazine shoot using Burnham in his roadster and Olson in his Hemi powered '32 coupe. Burnham had powered the roadster with a 321ci Pontiac but the rear end had such high gears it wouldn't spin the rear wheels easily. To get some action going we put dirt under the wheels so the tires would break loose. We had Burnham's daughter flag the rods off.

Below:  We used the Pleasanton train station to shoot
Burnham's Butterscotch Yellow roadster for the cover of
*Rod Action* magazine.  We gave him hell about his
yellow lettered tires but the 321ci Pontiac got it moving.

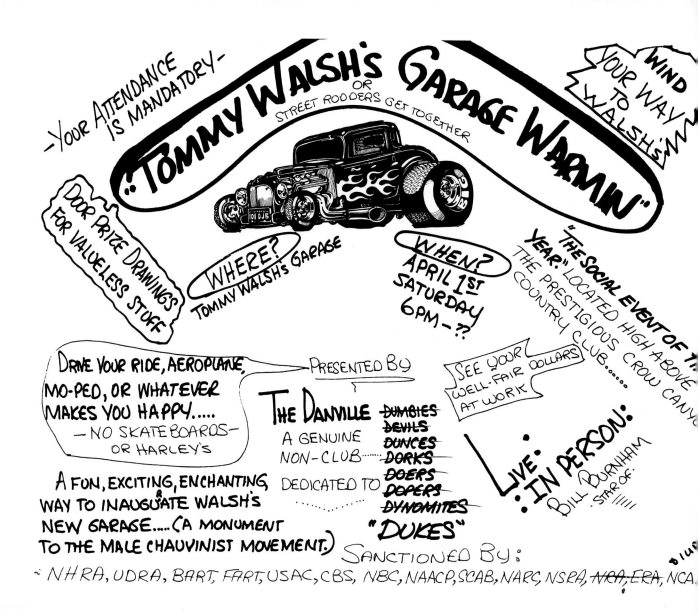

Above: The Dukes have always made it very clear what their focus was: Poke fun at life and have fun!

Right: The club house of the one and only Danville Dukes. Tommy Walsh, Bill Burnham, and me, at Walsh's place which became the club party garage. It was a huge space and perfect for get-togethers.

Their unbelievably successful first party was one of many blasts that followed. "Dukes' Doin's" became known as garage parties eventually and were timed to coincide with the Oakland Roadster Show, thereby drawing rodding celebrities from coast to coast. The celebrity roasts that followed were legendary and merciless. (Some celebs couldn't handle the heat and refused to return!)

Eventually Tommy's garage became too small to handle the growing crowds. To this day the many dozens of signatures on his white garage walls remain as a tribute to the many folks who have helped to formulate rodding as we know it today.

The luster may have worn off the annual ribald parties, barrels full of iced-down beer cans, sex ed. videos and a never-to-be-forgotten bus trip to Los Angeles—but the Dukes live on.

## The Dukes Today

The Dukes today barely resemble their 70's and 80's counterparts. However, the Dukes' break-fast meetings haven't missed a lick in some 18 years! Down through time they have outgrown some eateries and flat worn out their welcome at others. Every Saturday morning somewhere between 30 and 50 Dukes show up promptly at 8:00 a.m. for a session of criticism, nit-pickin', food fights and tire kicking. During decent weather it's not unusual to find at least 30 street rods in the restaurant parking lot being checked out by curious civilians.

With very few old-timer exceptions, the Dukes are comprised of an ever-changing unclub membership. Each Saturday seems like a revolving door with a few new guys gliding in, with an occasional old timer easing out. Many a first-time visitor has become a regular. As stuff

EXCLUSIVE, SELECTED, INVITED GUEST LIST INCLUDES:

THE WHO'S WHO OF Hot Street Rodding

ANDREW BRIZIO
TOM WALSH
DENNIS "LEG" DEBENEDICTIS
TEE CRAWFORD
MICKEY KNIGHT
RUDY PEREZ
DOCTOR MAGOO
DICK MENDONCA
JOHN HOLMES
WAYNE BLOECHL
RON HULSE
DAN PIMENTEL
CHICO HAGGEMAN
MERV HOAG
GOMER GOMES
STEVE MDAL
JIM ROBINSON
JOSE MAYALL
"PANCHO" MARTINEZ
PURE HELL GUASCO
ROGER GARCIA
HERNANDEZ
LARRY WESTERVELT
HITLER
DARRYL PACKARD
PINKY LEE
TEXAS SMITH
ED PINK
MONTANA JONES
DICK WILLIAMS
BIG ART BRANUM
CHUCK THORNDIKE
DEUCE OLSON
JIM WEARANGA
VINO JOE CARDOZA
BOB REYNOLDS
ANDY SOUTHARD
BRIAN HILL
ROGER STEELE
PAUL (MARC) FERREIRA
RICH GONZALES
DINO RAMACCIOTTI
LENNY MENDES
ED SANSONI
PAUL TUCKER
GARY GOODGUY
ED WATERS
BILLY BURNHAM
HUGO BROS
+ MANY OTHERS

# TROPHIES AWARDED FOR:

* **LONG DISTANCE** (OUT OF TOWNERS DON'T COUNT)
* **BEST BLUE PAINT** (BRING SAMPLE)
* **BEST UNBLOWN BUICK** (ONLY BLUE ONES)
* **BEST FAD "T"** ↝ TOP · BLOWER · + WHITEWALLS
* **MOST NOSTALGIC** (BURNHAM DOESN'T COUNT — EITHER DOES HAGEMANN)
* **OLDEST RODDER** (BURNHAM & HAGGEMANN STILL DON'T COUNT)
* **BEST SIGN** (☞ DOESN'T COUNT)

**ENTERTAINMENT!**

ROD IN ACTION MOVIES (LOOPS)
BENCH RACIN
BULL SHITTIN
SHUCKIN & JIVIN
LIE SWAPPING & CHEATING
SKATE BOARD RACIN'
SLIDES

**REQUIREMENTS**

BRING:
#1 $1.00 FOR DOOR PRIZE DRAWING
#2 YOUR WALLET w/ DRIVERS LICENSE (NOT TO PROVE YOUR AGE BUT TO PROVE YOU ARE REALLY YOU)
#3 PINK SLIP — FOOD STAMPS — DIRTY PICTURES
#4 SLEEPING BAG — CASE YOU GET BORED
#5 ASPIRIN AND/OR MIDOL

=YOU MUST ATTEND=

HORS D'OEUVRES (FANCY NAME FOR CHIPS, NUTS, + PRETZELS)

BEER 35¢
SODA 35¢
WINE 44

happens, the irreverent parody on car clubs has lost some of its sting. The original coveted Dukes T-shirts disappeared, replaced by the once-ridiculed club jacket. Hundred of Dukes club plaques now adorn rods across the U.S.

Yet, despite the jackets and plaques, the group remains, amazingly, totally unstructured. The mere suggestion of anything resembling a rule or regulation is met with a hail of humiliating jeers and a barrage of coffee creamers.

The tiny handful of individuals who have attempted to convert the Dukes into "a real car club" have found themselves in treacherous and terribly unfriendly territory.

Each year at the Goodguys West Coast Nationals at Pleasanton, California, the fellows and general public can be seen participating in the annual Dukes Shade Tree Social. A couple of hundred collector Dukes T-shirts disappear in an instant.

The three original Dukes are almost always on hand at this Goodguys event to reminisce about the past and expound upon the two main themes that have made the Danville Dukes a natural and national success—support of the rebel that exists in every rodder and club meetings that are never called to order—because nothing can take the spontaneous and laid-back fun out of rodding any faster than rules, order and regulations.

Below: Burnham is always out to have good time. Here he is posing for our first Goodguys Swimsuit edition. A dashing devil, eh!

FOR GOODNESS SA

MERCED

DUKE, DUKE, DUKE

HENR

—AND THE WINNER, BILL HOGUE!

EYE JUST CAN'T BELIEVE MY HIBOY DIDN'T WIN!

Over THE HILL Gang

BILL HOGUE'S RED-ROSE THAT GO

This Dave Bell cartoon first appeared in *Street Rodder* in January '84, after the '83 Western Nationals in Merced. Bell's illustration depicts Burnham grinning like a monkey! I love this kind of cartoon work that Bell has been drawing for *Street Rodder* since March, '74 which has got to be some kind of record! (Thanks to Dave Bell and *Street Rodder* for the use of the cartoon.)

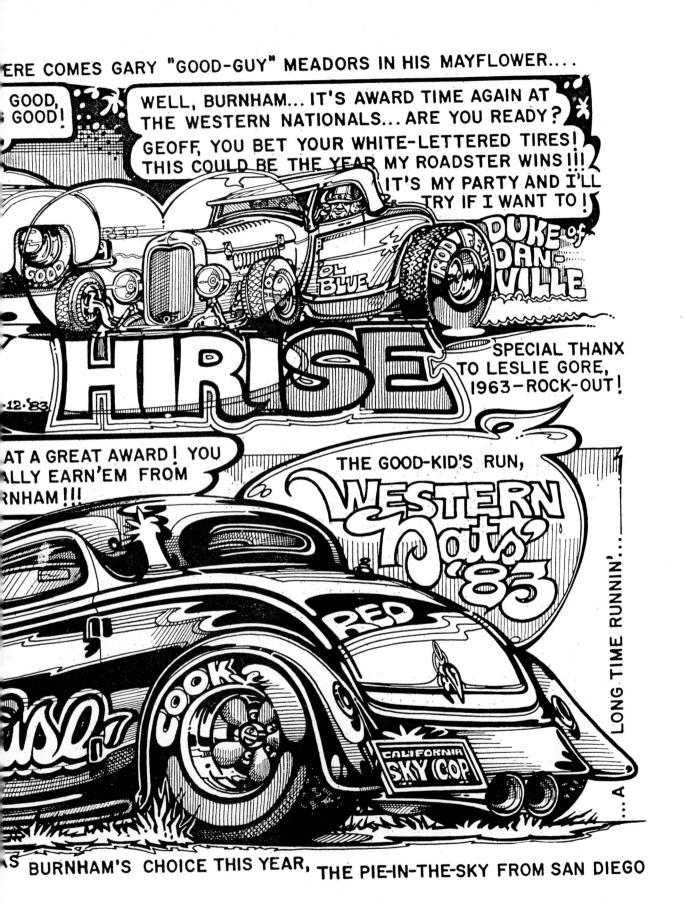

# The Goodguys Garage

I've been building cars since I was in high school and continue to work on many of my own machines in the garage at home. Like all rodders, I get a great deal of satisfaction and pleasure from this work, plus the enjoyment of driving the beast on the street. My favorite is still the Plymouth which replicates the car I drove to high school and the photos which follow involve many of the cars I have built over the past 40 years.

Marty and the kid next door helped me put a new Chrysler six into the Plymouth. I paid $100 for this car at a wrecking yard in Livermore and drove it home. The body was not too bad; I managed to save the front fenders but had to replace the rears. There was very little rust in the car so there was no backtracking to repair it before we started recreating my old high school ride.

Above: The '32 is under conversion from a full-fendered to a fenderless highboy. At the same time, Marc and I were building this Cal-Look VW with a 2-inch chopped top, an early hood and deck lid, '37 Ford headlights and Porsche wheels. It was eventually painted in Porsche red.

Right: I drove this Blazer for years. It was lightly customized with stepped A-arms and a reworked rear end to get the body down low. I later had it scalloped but it was then stolen and never recovered.

Above: The '32 had real knock-off wheels at this stage and they were a pain. They would back off every 100 miles, so we had to stop to hammer them back on. I was in L.A. with the car and went to Woody Gilmore's shop on Chuck Lombardo's advice. Woody fixed the problem with a little set screw. Later on, after I had the wheels widened an inch, one blew apart at about 70 mph on I-5 north of Sacramento. No damage to me or the car, luckily.

Left: Marty and I rebuilt the ' 53 Ford Pickup which we'd owned for 15 to 20 years. As usual, it was something different, with a 318 Dodge, and a 727 Torqueflite tranny, a Chevelle front end, and painted in Chevrolet Huggar Orange.

Below: Marty (left), Marc (middle), and me on the right in about 1992 putting a fresh motor in the '32 while we refreshed the Tudor from front to rear. We also had the front end resprayed after turning 100,000 miles, visiting 41 states and Canada.

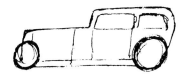

Soooo Low
CDan

LOW BOY CHASSIS
LONG 4 BARS
VEGA STEERING
SUPER ZOOMIE HEAD LITE BRACKETS
4 BAR BRACKETS IN FRAME NOT HANGING DOWN
ENGINE & TRANS MOUNTS HIGH
FRAME RAILS SUCKED IN AT FRONT
STUBBED NOSE
GRILLE SHELL 2½" 3" FURTHER FRONT
& DROPPED 1" TO ALLOW FOR SLIGHTLY SLOPED HOOD
FORD REAR END CENTERED
COIL OVERS MOUNTED IN FRONT OF R.E. TO ALLOW
ROOM FOR GAS TANK TO BE BUILT INSIDE REAR
ROLLED PAN
RUN BRAKE LINES
MOUNT BODY
INSTALL TILT COLUMN
HOOK UP STEERING
EXHAUST
"ROLLER" W/ BRAKES & STEERING

Here are the two pages of ideas and instructions which I
drew up when I decided what I really wanted out of the
"Soooo Low CDan."

STUFF

HIDDEN DOOR HINGES
REMOVE COWL LIP
   "     SHELL    "
3 PIECE SOLID HOOD w/ BODY LINE & CONCELED LATCHS
   OR HINGED AT FRONT

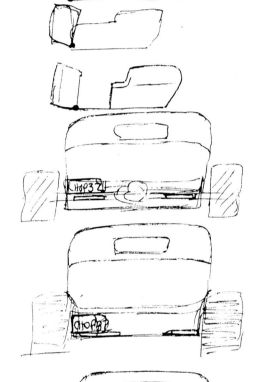

ROLLED REAR PAN
CAD LITES
OR ½ PONTIAC LITES (LONGER)
FLIP DOWN LIC. W/ FILLER BEHIND
FUEL TANK

MEHIUCH

14" x 6" WHEELS FRONT w/ SHORT TIRES
15" x 9"   "   REAR w/ TALL & FAT TIRES
                ↑ NOT "TOO" TALL

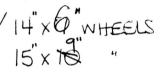

TANK
PAN

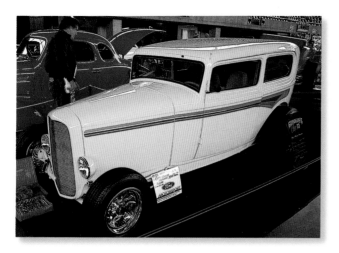

Above: The '32, which I'd finished the year before, was in the Oakland Roadster Show in 1987 where it was put in the center arena. By this time the '32 had gone through four transformations.

Right: I gave the Tudor the title of the "Soooo Low CDan" after it had been through three complete updates or rebuilds. The '32 became the basis of our Goodguys logo and is seen on all our Goodguys products from one angle or another. All sorts of folks did work on the "CDan" including Magoo and Sam Foose.

Above: This is how the Plymouth looked just after it was first assembled. My buddies would come by the house and give me all kinds of free advice like, "What are you doing with this piece of ----?" At a party I got into a conversation with Weldon Ballard and Rich Roberts from Merced about my old Plymouth. They knew my car because of its white upholstery with silver welts, and mentioned they'd seen what was left of it in Gene Horns' wrecking yard in Fresno just a few week earlier. I went to Gene's and looked over what was still there. The only salvable part was the hood, which was louvered. I bought it for the new car but still had to hunt around for a pair of NOS rear fenders and a couple of good gravel pans.

Right: The Plymouth has turned out much better than the first one I built in high school. It drives just fine, has dropped spindles, a cool sounding exhaust, and looks just like I always wanted it to look. I finally got the height and the ride just right which was something I never achieved with the first edition.

We have let the yellow theme evolve a little in the past few rods. Marilyn's Foose-built, Brizio chassised, '34 roadster is finished in metallic plum purple and rolls on Boyds billet wheels. It is capped with a removable Carson-style top which is trimmed in gray fabric.

We never set out to find a '51 Nash Airflyte convertible, it just happened. We found it, loved it, and slammed it with a Mustang II front end, added a Chevy V6, and now we drive it. This past summer we drove it all over the mid-West from Texas to Indy and beyond. That's Miss Jones and me!

I always liked these '56 Lincoln Mark II's. This one turned out great after a struggle to get it built. The basic body was handled by Denny Olson and Al Swedberg with a custom chassis created out of Ford running gear by Hot Rod Enterprises. All the finish work and paint was done down at Sam Foose's shop in Solvang, California. Denny had Cope Brothers Machine build a mild 460 cubic inch Lincoln for the car which is mated to a Ford C-6 transmission. The car appeared on the cover of *Custom Rodder* in March, '95.

I purchased this custom Chevy Caprice wagon from MoonEyes USA in Santa Fe Springs. They had built it up in Moon Yellow which is the same yellow as Goodguys' Yellow, I discovered. Dean Moon picked '56 Ford Sunflower Yellow off his Ford Station Wagon as his Moon Yellow at about the same time I picked the same color for my Plymouth. When we got the wagon we repainted the rear quarters and added the Goodguys logos. The Caprice is now used every day for Goodguys business and everyone loves to drive it.

# The Goodguys Today

As hot rodding was getting its second wind in the early 70's, rods were coming out of the woodwork. There were far more of them than most of us had imagined and consequently a group of us in the San Francisco area formed the "Nor-Cal Early Iron Car Club" in 1971, patterned after car clubs of the 50's.

Nor-Cal Early Iron decided to throw a two-day party at the Lodi Fairgrounds in California. Why not? Andy Brizio had been hosting his successful "Andy's Picnic" for a few years. We decided to give it a try—but we weren't too sure how to get the deal off the ground. I went and talked with Mel Fernandez, manager of the Oakland

Opposite Page: The flyer for our first full scale "The Goodguys West Coast Nationals" in August 1987. We made it a three-day show with a Hot Rod Drag event at Fremont, driving events, entertainment and a Magoo Give-a-way '29 Hi-boy roadster kit.

**ATTENTION STREET RODDERS!**
This is NOT an NSRA Event

**GOODGUY'S**

## AUGUST
### 14 · 15 · 16 · 1987

# WEST COAST NATIONALS

# PLEASANTON FAIRGROUNDS
## PLEASANTON, CALIFORNIA

**1000's of STREET RODS & HOT RODS** ★ **100's of MANUFACTURERS & SUPPLIERS**
**100's of MODEL CARS** ★ **A GIANT ARTS/CRAFTS SHOW**

*Rock*

CHUCK RIO &
THE CHAMPS
"Tequila"

THE DIAMONDS
"Lil Darlin"

*and*

THE DRIFTERS
"There Goes My Baby"

DONNIE BROOKS
"Mission Bells"

*Roll!*

*Plus . . .*

**NDRA**

**Hot Rod Drags**

FRI
NITE
AT
BAYLANDS

**DRIVING EVENTS** ★ **PARTIES** ★ **WINERY TOURS**
**DANCES** ★ **HOT AIR BALLOON RIDES** ★ **GAMES**
**CAMPING** ★ **NON-STOP FUN!**

**GRAND PRIZE**
A Magoo '29 HiBoy Roadster Kit
w/all the Components Necessary to Assemble It

**PLUS** an All Expense Paid Weekend
at the 1988 West Coast Nationals
celebrating your completion
of the Roadster.

**STREET RODDER** MAGAZINE

**THE STREET RODDING EVENT OF THE DECADE!**
FOR INFO:  WEST COAST NATIONALS, P.O. BOX 424, ALAMO, CA 94507, (415) 838-9876

**SREA**
STREET ROD EQUIPMENT ASSOCIATION

101

Roadster Show. He said; "You'll never be able to pull it off!" That was all the incentive I needed, the word never isn't in my vocabulary. Looking back, I can see now that we were confronting the traditional indoor car show with our ideas for a huge outdoor drive-in exhibition. Nonetheless, with the help of many of my club member friends we did it, and in grand style.

I sold ads for the show, enabling my brother Craig and I to put together a neat program with a bright purple cover theme: "Lodi— Have A Grape Day" as Lodi is one of California's major table grape and wine centers.

Five hundred and sixty-six hot rods

> I knew Tom McMullen for years, first by his hot rods that I saw in the magazines and then from his own magazines. Over the years I got to know him and when he did the School Bus Rod, he and Deanna brought the bus up to Pleasanton where it was a great hit, as it had just appeared on the cover of *Street Rodder* magazine.

showed up for the first Nor-Cal rod run. We had a sit-down dinner for all the participants and the event registration package was a mere $10. (This was long before county fairgrounds discovered how lucrative hot rod runs could be!)

The club did very well on that first event, maybe a bit too well. There was a big blow up about what to do with the money we made and it seemed like half the club members knew a tax lawyer and the other half wanted to be one.

My idea was to use the money to buy the club's entry into the next Andy's Picnic but that idea didn't set too well. The next year I organized "Lodi" to be held under the banner of the newly formed Northern California Street Rod Association, a group of 13 street rod clubs. The 1974 event was even bigger.

These Lodi events ultimately gave me the confidence I needed. I loved rods and customs, I was a good organizer and could make stuff happen. In December 1974 I found enough time between my regular job with Carter/ Wallace and my car hobbies to be the Show Chairman of the San Francisco Cow Palace Car Show. The Cow Palace deal had all the big names behind it like Bill Moeller, Blackie Gejeian, "Baggy" Bagdasarian and Daryl Starbird. I think I did just about everything but judge the cars and M.C. the awards ceremonies.

Shortly after the Cow Palace show Carter/Wallace handed me a promotion and transferred me to Tennessee. It was there at the company that the moniker "Goodguy" was hung around my neck. I had established a new series of attractive incentives for the sales force and I guess they figured I was a pretty "good guy" and called me so. My brief stint in Tennessee led to my contact with the National Street Rod Association owners Gilbert Bugg and Vernon Walker.

A year later Carter/Wallace transferred me back to California with yet another promotion. When I returned it was obvious that the West Coast could support a national rod run of its own and with that thought I approached Vernon and Bugg. I proposed a business deal in which I would do all the work to establish the event under the NSRA banner and consequently produced the first "Western Nationals" at Merced, California in 1978.

This was a super deal, drawing 1400 cars. A year later Gilbert and Vernon asked me to try my hand at the Nats East in Timonium, Maryland. I took it over and the event was a success but the location wasn't good enough.

Our Pacific Northwest Rod and Custom Nationals in Puyallup, Washington, attracts a great crowd each year in the middle of June. Of course we have it then when it's not raining.

The following year we moved the Nats to York, Pennsylvania, and it took off like a rocket.

All the while York and Merced were being produced I was doing Mini-Nats in Yuba City and Ventura, California. We were setting up events everywhere, flying all over the place. I remember one time, arriving home exhausted in the morning, Marilyn and I crashed into bed, and woke up to discover we'd left our briefcase with the entire event proceeds outside the front door!

All the street rod event work was planned in our house during the week nights and not only were we constantly flying across country, I was still working full time. It was tough to juggle everything and make it work. Then the word came from Carter/Wallace: "If you want to progress with this rapidly growing company a move to Cranberry, New Jersey, might be necessary." It was time to make a career decision.

We were pretty close to making financial ends meet doing the rodding events so I decided to resign although I had a few sleepless nights thinking about it.

We made a deal with NSRA to do all their regional events, and they would take over the registration and mailing. We also organized a few of our own "Goodguys Get-Togethers" and worked hard to make it all happen.

In 1984 we staged events in Des Moines, Iowa; Knoxville, Tennessee; York, Pennsylvania, and Merced, California. Charlie Rose was doing a great job at the Nats North so we weren't involved up there. In 1987 we decided to take our Goodguys enterprise very seriously. We wanted folks to understand that the Goodguys was a separate and independent hot rod entity.

I came up with the thought that early 50's Chevys, Fords, Mercs, Studes and so forth, shouldn't be excluded from our rodding events. Those rodded and customized cars, along with fat fendered hot rods, comprised the vast majority of what guys were driving in the mid-fifties.

Even burning a little rubber was no big sin when done at the right place at the right time and safely sanctioned hot rod drag racing would be allowed. The idea for a "Nostalgia Drag Racing" event evolved in 1984 and was promoted by the California Vintage Rods Club at the Fremont strip. The following year our Nor Cal Early Iron Club tried a nostalgia race, but only a few cars showed up.

The venue for the "Western Nationals" in 1985 was in San Jose at the Santa Clara County Fairgrounds. The retired pro drag racer, Tom Prufer, held a Friday night drag race at Fremont as a prelude. It turned out okay but by today's standards it was really no big deal. I knew nostalgia races had the potential of being part of the hot rod scene but recognized that a lot more effort and promotion would be necessary to make it a hit.

In 1987 I promoted a nostalgia race at Fremont in conjunction with the First West Coast Nationals event in nearby Pleasanton, California. I booked Tom Topping and Jim Davis to match-race their front motored top fuelers. About 40 other guys also made the scene to run their old race cars, and a huge crowd of 4,000 rodding spectators showed up. I remember Terry Kniss, the Fremont strip operator, asking how could we pull in such a crowd with our nothing' little antique drag race when he couldn't get a crowd for his real drag races? Even the Highway Patrol had shown up because traffic was so snarled and backed up on the freeway.

In 1989 we inaugurated the first nostalgia Jim Davis Memorial Drag Race at Sears Point Raceway. Jim Davis's son Brent had been severely injured in a racing incident and barely a few months later Jim, the Bay Area's most popular, colorful and innovative drag racer had lost his life in a motorcycle accident. The Memorial race was my first attempt at recreating

Ed Roth has always amazed me, not only is his work so creative and energetic, he's funny and always on the go. Ed will drive 1,500 miles, do a show, sleep in his pickup for two nights and then drive home again right after the show. Here's Roth and me at Puyallup, Washington, just before the show opened.

the excitement of drag racing and street hot rodding that I remembered as the best times of my life.

Prior to this, I'd been working with The National Hot Rod Association conducting some old time drag races at Indianapolis Raceway Park (IRP). I was negotiating with Bob Daniels, manager of IRP, but scheduling was a big problem. Finally, in the summer of 1989, I got a firm deal at NHRA's 1/4 mile-Mecca of drag racing at Indy.

We called it "The Goodguys Hot Rod Happening." It was a combination of a national rod run and drag racing, all at the same facility. We featured Mindy Fry, Art Chrisman and Jerry Moreland with their cars. But what happened? It rained! Only 600 cars showed up and our hopes

"Gary's been a fantastic ambassador for street rodding."

# Herb Martinez

This photo shows the Tom Topping unblown A/Fuel dragster which we helped sponsor for a while. Tom owned the car and had Brooks Brown drive it for him. The car was very fast and held both ends of the record for quite a while.

were dashed and drowned.

But we knew the event and idea was still good so we shelved our losses and tried again. Persistence prevailed and now "The Indy Hot Rod Nationals" draws almost 5,000 rods and race cars.

We attacked nostalgia racing in Bakersfield, California, with a vengeance, too. I had attended many races at "Bakerspatch," especially for the March Meet in the late 50's and I envisioned a spectacular rod and race car turnout for that facility.

In 1996 we chalked up the biggest "Nostalgia" drag race ever. Hundreds of rods, customs and muscle cars showed up to show off, and hundreds of nostalgia racers brought their cars to race. However, Bakersfield was no overnight sensation by any means. It was one of those deals that took almost ten years and a few bottles of red ink to finally materialize.

The Goodguys' approach to rods, customs and racing was, and maybe still is, controversial. Bad weather like rain or unbearable heat results in a dollar disaster but that's just a given and a risky part of the game.

The greater risk however is bucking street rodding's "city hall" and those many respected friends who have all their eggs in the pre-'49 basket.

We feel at least partially responsible for bringing respectability to the words "hot rod!" Likewise, we bucked a solid 15 years of ingrained tradition by welcoming shoebox rods and customs to our events. Why not? They were a huge and integral part, maybe even the predominant force, of the middle 50's rodding scene. The very roots of rodding could no longer be shunned, ignored or swept under the table.

We have never believed that drag racing, dry lakes contests, and circle track roaring roadsters ought to be relegated to selective memories and the dusty shelves and shadows of history. We broke some rules and we're glad we

It's amazing what folks bring to our events! This flamed winged baby buggy is just gorgeous.

did. We must have done some things right because the growth of the Goodguys has been phenomenal.

Today, we have a full-time staff of 24 people and a modest volunteer group of another three dozen or so dedicated guys and gals across the country. We produce 25 to 30 events a year and are about as maxed out as we can get. We try to do a better job with each of our events to make them exciting for the rod owning participant, exhibitor, and those spectators who rightfully expect an entertaining day or weekend.

We think our drive-in, car owning participants deserve a full schedule of "eventful" activities while spectators who walk through the gates are provided with a "show." Let the other organizations standardize—we feel that different facilities and automotive concepts need variable, not standardized, rules, regulations and attention.

In Perry, Georgia, the beautiful fairgrounds have a huge car capacity, and we have opened it up to later models with a mixture of pre- and post- 49 cars. Pleasanton's facility will hold a lot of cars too, but hotel facilities are limited so we currently cut dates off at 1954 and earlier.

Drag Racing events are completely different and we have established the perfect cut-off date, 1972, as the year that front-motored top fuelers and the last true muscle cars were built. The muscle car or marque car guys have their own events but we still invite them all to our Get-Togethers and they show up in droves.

We don't judge their cars, we "pick 'em" which is one reason why I think our "Goodguys Get-Togethers" are so popular. Any year, make or model of American-manufactured or American-powered vehicle is welcome. Our 1996 Spring Get-Together was the all-time biggest spectator turnout in our history.

Sometimes our spectators return a year or so later with a hot rod, custom, race car or muscle car of their own. When a guy approached me one day with the advice: "Gary, your job is to make sure more new and young guys get into this hobby. Don't forget that!" I realized that this is probably why The Goodguys haven't standardized a program. Car enthusiasts are not firmly locked into one specific make or model vehicle. A Deuce owner may get cranked up when he sees a Camaro like the one he owned in 1968 or someone with a Roadrunner may spot a '32 Plymouth coupe that gets his juices boiling. Dozens, if not hundreds, of pre-'49 hot rod purists are currently wrenching away on a '51 Olds or a '53 Merc, just like the one they always wanted back in the 50's. I like to think that being open to the diversity of the hot car hobby is one of the reasons why the Goodguys organization is busting out at the seams.

"Street is Swell, at Goodguys shows - El Polacko."

# Norm Grabowski

Cruising the Indy 500 track with Mindy Fry in her roadster at the First Indy Goodguys Hot Rod Nationals. This event is now eight years old and one of our most popular events.

West Coast Nationals at the fairgrounds in Pleasanton, California, is
one of the most delightful locations
for a hot rod event.  It has great lawns
on which to park and picnic,  plenty of
shade, and great facilities for display-
ing rods and entertaining folks.

Below: This hot little modified valve cover racer built by Doug Silva is typical of some of the neat stuff that participants created for the valve cover racers.

To create more fun and interest as a family event we have promoted many special interest happenings. Over the years we have had all kinds of features including creeper races, beauty contests and model car competitions. The Valve Cover Races seen here at Pleasanton have been very popular, with folks bringing the wildest array of valve covers to races.

For the past ten years we have put together a series of Goodguys Giveaway Rods with a mass of street rod industry support. This is the Giveaway Vicky which Jerry and Muffy Williams built into their dream rod in 1993. I liked Jerry's one word when he won the Vicky. "Awesome!"

Cruising events are part of the fun and if it's not some hairy sounding machine making its way through the crowd, you're just as likely to see a nifty nostalgia T-bucket like this one roll by.

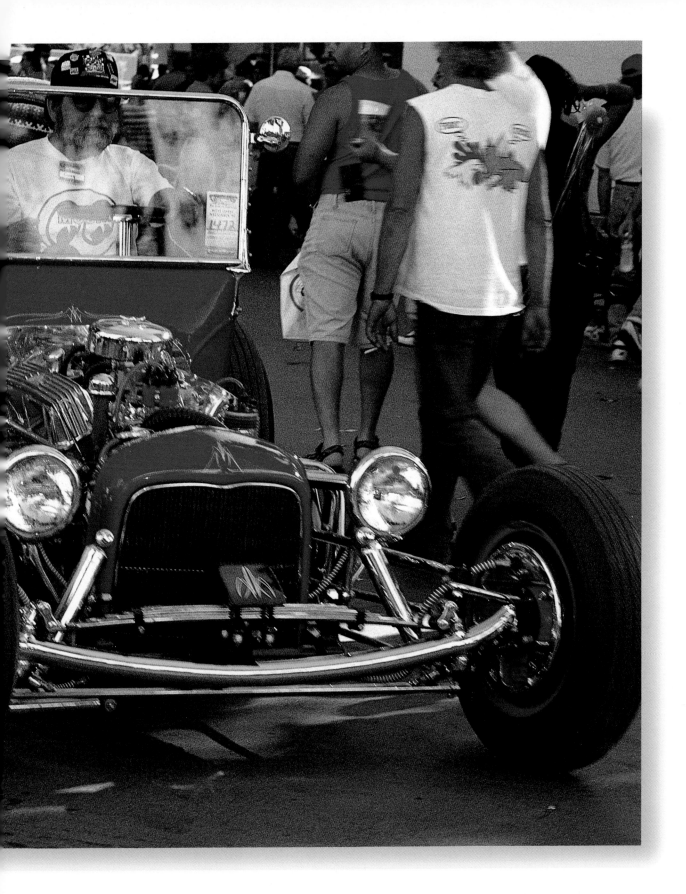

Above: It's amazing what arrives in the mail sometimes.
Check out this envelope.

Far Right: We send out a mass of Christmas cards every
year and if you aren't on our mailing list here's a sample of
the fun we have had.

"I have a good time with the people at Goodguys'
events and Gary is always there."

## Gene Winfield

We were the first hot rod organization to display Plymouth's new Prowler hot rod. This slick machine is set to do wonders for the image of hot rodding and I look forward to having the opportunity to have a good thrash in another one sometime soon.

At the World of Speed event run by the Utah Salt Racing Association in September 1994 on Bonneville Salt Flats, I got my 200 mph Club record in the Goodguys' streamliner owned and built by Ed Hagerty and Dave Dozier. The car gave me a 223.220 mph record as the World's Fastest Blown Flathead on gas. It is powered by a 1939, 323ci, eight-cylinder Chrysler flathead.

Left:  I think the game is called "Balls Up Mother Brown!" It was played by the Willys guys last year as part of the fun out in the Willys Round-Up area at the West Coast Nationals.

Below:  Over the years we promoted a series of VW events including the Bug Bash, Super VW Sunday and Bugs by the Bay.  These shows have been at Sears Point Raceway and at the fairgrounds in Vallejo, San Jose, Ventura, Pomona, Pleasanton and even Merced.

Right:   Art Chrisman and his magnificent "Hustler" dragster have always put on a great show for the crowd at our nostalgia drag racing events.  I first saw this machine back in the fifties racing at Bakersfield so I feel a close association with it as it has now been part of my drag racing adventures for about 40 years.

"Gary's a true hot rodder and he realizes what hot rodders want when they come to an event."

## Roy Brizio

The popularity of nostalgia drag racing continues to build. Over the years we have had some great competitors. Recently we have featured the newly remodeled "Hurst Hemi Under Glass," seen leaping skyward at the Jim Davis Memorial Nitro Nationals at Sears Point, California.

# Index